MY MOST
FABULOUS
FANTASTIC
RECIPES

·Doily Publishing Incorporated·

MY MOST FABULOUS FANTASTIC RECIPES

Published by Doily Publishing Inc.

ISBN   1-895292-22-0

The fantastic cover and
hand lettering done by
· Kim La Fave ·

·Printed and produced in Canada by Centax Books·

We may live
        without friends,
We may live
        without books,
But civilized man
        cannot live
without cooks!

(Bulwer-Lytton)

INDEX

Mark especially scrumptious stuff with a ♡:

CHEESE STRAWS

1 scant cup all-purpose flour
Pinch cayenne pepper
1/2 cup butter

1/4 cup milk
1 can finely grated sharp Cheddar cheese

In a medium bowl, using your fingers, rub together flour, cayenne pepper and butter until mixture is crumbly and resembles oatmeal. Make a well in the centre and add milk and cheese. Mix into a rough dough; form into a ball and wrap in plastic wrap. Chill in refrigerator for at least an hour to ease rolling out. When ready to bake, roll out on a lightly floured surface to form a large rectangle about 1/4-inch thick. With a sharp knife or pastry cutter, cut dough into straws about 1/2-inch wide and about 3 inches long.

Arrange on ungreased baking sheet and bake 12 to 15 minutes in a pre-heated 400°F oven or until just barely golden brown. Cool on wire rack. Carefully package in bright holiday baking tin or sturdy box to prevent breakage. Attach a note with instructions to reheat in a slow oven (250°) for about 5 minutes.

Makes about 3 dozen.

Page

21. _____
22. _____
23. _____
24. _____
25. _____
26. _____
27. _____
28. _____
29. _____
30. _____
31. _____
32. _____
33. _____
34. _____
35. _____
36. _____
37. _____
38. _____
39. _____
40. _____
41. _____
42. _____

Page

43.

44.

45.

46.

47.

48.

49.

50.

51.

52.

53.

54.

55.

56.

57.

58.

59.

60.

61.

62.

63.

64.

Page

65. _____

66. _____

67. _____

68. _____

69. _____

70. _____

71. _____

72. _____

73. _____

74. _____

75. _____

76. _____

77. _____

78. _____

79. _____

80. _____

81. _____

82. _____

83. _____

84. _____

85. _____

86. _____

Page.
87. _____
88. _____
89. _____
90. _____
91. _____
92. _____
93. _____
94. _____
95. _____
96. _____
97. _____
98. _____
99. _____
100. _____
101. _____
102. _____
103. _____
104. _____
105. _____
106. _____
107. _____
108. _____

Page
109. _____
110. _____
111. _____
112. _____
113. _____
114. _____
115. _____
116. _____
117. _____
118. _____
119. _____
120. _____
121. _____
122. _____
123. _____
124. _____
125. _____
126. _____
127. _____
128. _____
129. _____
130. _____

Page

ingredients

method

ingredients

method

ingredients

method

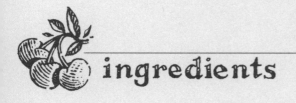

ingredients

method

ingredients

method

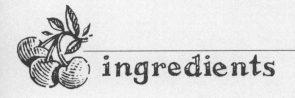

ingredients

method

ingredients

method

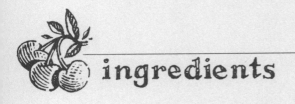# ingredients

method

ingredients

method

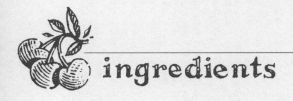 ingredients

method

ingredients

method

 # ingredients

method

ingredients

method

ingredients

method

ingredients

method

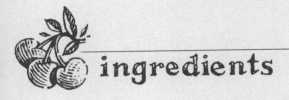

ingredients

method

ingredients

method

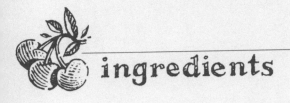

ingredients

method

ingredients

method

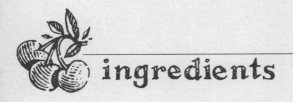 ingredients

method

ingredients

method

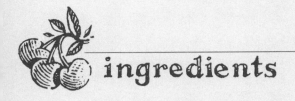 ingredients

method

ingredients

method

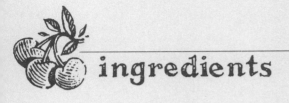 ingredients

method

Page _____

ingredients

method

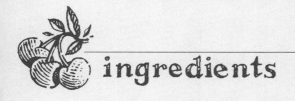

ingredients

method

ingredients

method

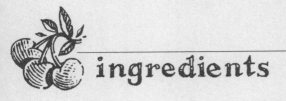

ingredients

method

Page ____

ingredients

method

 **ingredients**

method

ingredients

method

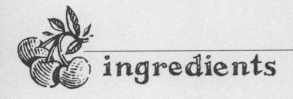 ingredients

method

ingredients

method

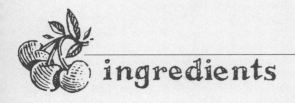 ## ingredients

method

ingredients

method

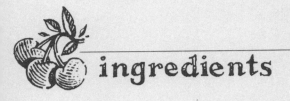

ingredients

method

ingredients

method

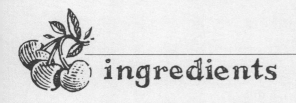 ingredients

method

ingredients

method

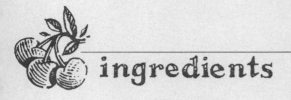

ingredients

method

_____

_____

_____

_____

_____

_____

_____

_____

_____

_____

_____

_____

_____

_____

_____

ingredients

method

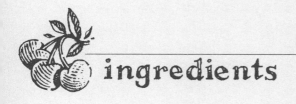

ingredients

method

ingredients

method

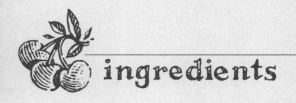 ingredients

method

ingredients

method

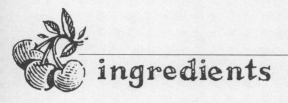 ingredients

method

ingredients

method

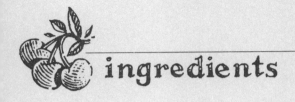 ingredients

method

ingredients

method

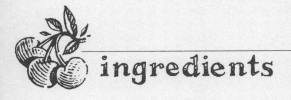 # ingredients

method

ingredients

method

ingredients

method

_____

_____

_____

_____

_____

_____

_____

_____

_____

_____

_____

_____

_____

_____

_____

ingredients

method

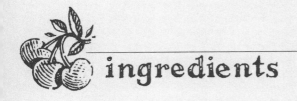 ingredients

method

ingredients

method

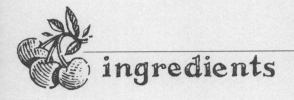

ingredients

method

ingredients

method

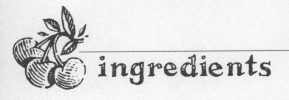

ingredients

method

ingredients

method

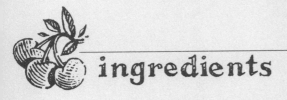 # ingredients

method

ingredients

method

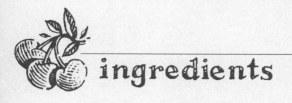

ingredients

method

ingredients

method

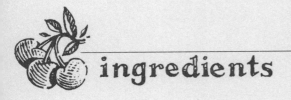# ingredients

method

ingredients

method

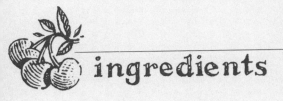

ingredients

method

ingredients

method

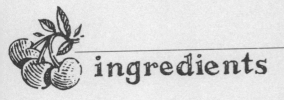 ingredients

method

ingredients

method

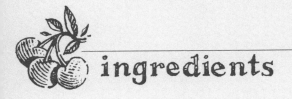

ingredients

method

ingredients

method

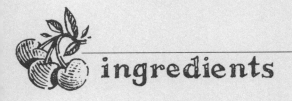

ingredients

method

ingredients

method

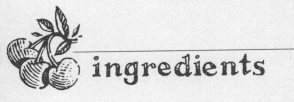 **ingredients**

method

ingredients

method

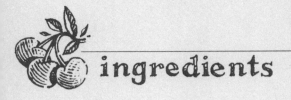

ingredients

method

ingredients

method

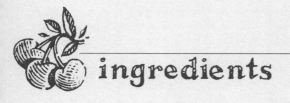

ingredients

method

ingredients

method

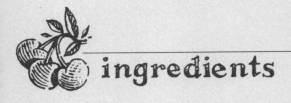 # ingredients

method

ingredients

method

 ingredients

method

ingredients

method

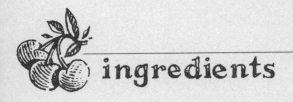 ingredients

method

_____

_____

_____

_____

_____

_____

_____

_____

_____

_____

_____

_____

_____

_____

ingredients

method

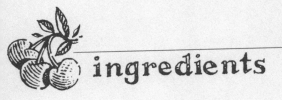 # ingredients

method

ingredients

method

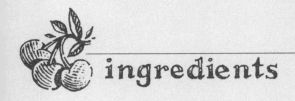 ingredients

method

ingredients

method

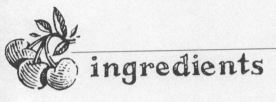

ingredients

method

ingredients

method

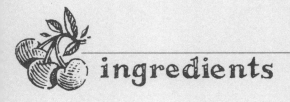

ingredients

method

ingredients

method

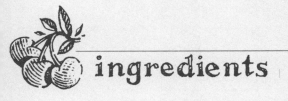

ingredients

method

ingredients

method

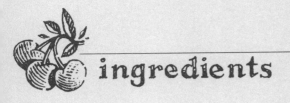

ingredients

method

ingredients

method

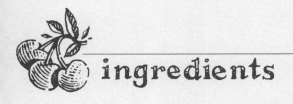 ingredients

method

ingredients

method

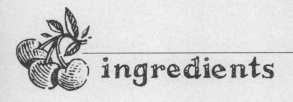

ingredients

method

ingredients

method

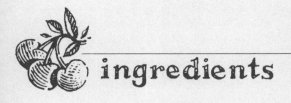

ingredients

method

ingredients

method

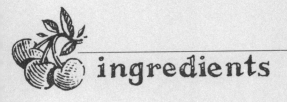# ingredients

method

ingredients

method

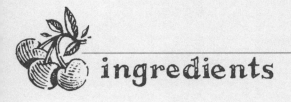

ingredients

method

ingredients

method

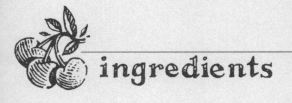

ingredients

method

ingredients

method

ingredients

method

ingredients

method

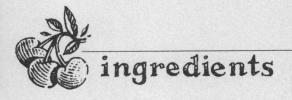# ingredients

method

ingredients

method

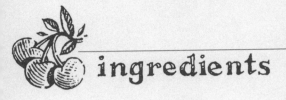

ingredients

method

ingredients

method

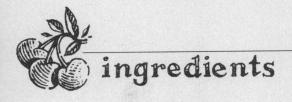 ingredients

method

ingredients

method

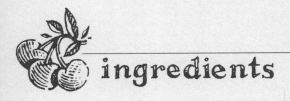 ingredients

method

ingredients

method

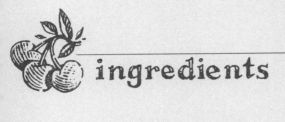# ingredients

method

_____
_____
_____
_____
_____
_____
_____
_____
_____
_____
_____
_____
_____
_____
_____
_____
_____

ingredients

method

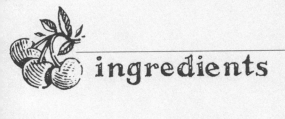

ingredients

method

_____

_____

_____

_____

_____

_____

_____

_____

_____

_____

_____

_____

_____

_____

_____

ingredients

method

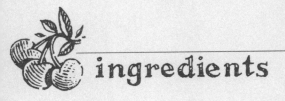 ## ingredients

method

ingredients

method

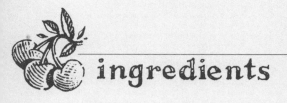

ingredients

method

ingredients

method

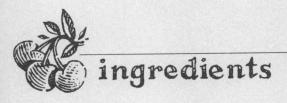

ingredients

method

ingredients

method

ingredients

method

ingredients

method

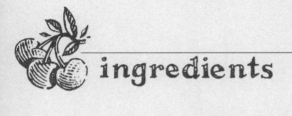

ingredients

method

ingredients

method

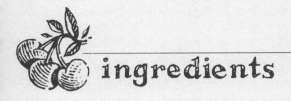

ingredients

method

ingredients

method

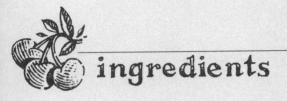 ingredients

method

ingredients

method

 **ingredients**

method

ingredients

method

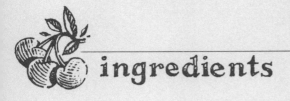 ingredients

method

ingredients

method

 ingredients

method

ingredients

method

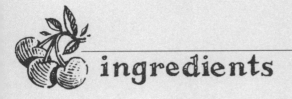 ingredients

method

ingredients

method

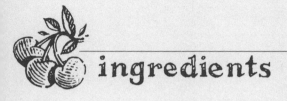 ingredients

method

ingredients

method

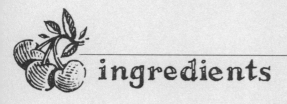# ingredients

method

To order additional copies

My Most Fabulous
Fantastic Recipes. $11.95
Postage and handling . . . . $ 2.50
Subtotal . . . . _____
In Canada, add 7 % GST . . _____
Total enclosed . . . . _____
U.S. Orders payable in U.S. funds

Name :_____
Street :_____
City :_____ Prov./state :_____
Country :_____ Postal code :_____

Please make cheque or money order
payable to:

DOILY PUBLISHING
GENERAL DELIVERY
ROBERTS CREEK
BRITISH COLUMBIA
VON • 2WO